THE BOOK OF WATER SPIRITS

BENITO TORRES

CONTENT

<u>ACKNOWLEDGMENTS</u>

I would like to thank all those teachers
whose teachings have made this book come
to life, it could not have been written
without their help.

INTRODUCTION:

This book is a continuation of my work *"The rituals of Mami Wata."* This is an improved and extended version, with new rituals added, which include the evocation of many more water spirits. This new book arises from the need to answer the many questions I have received by email since the publication of *The Rituals of Mami Wata.*

The rituals described in this book were deliberately omitted from my earlier work because they require supervision by a guru or subject matter expert, all this to guarantee the physical and spiritual safety of the practitioner during the ceremony. But due to the constant request from the readers and after a long reflection I have decided to transmit them to the general public.

I have also decided to create a *Youtube channel* so that readers can listen to the correct pronunciation of the ritual mantras, the link to which is in the last section of this book, along with my new email address. Those people who have questions or need guidance on some rituals can contact me and I will help them completely free of charge.

However, readers must be reminded that the rituals offered in my books are extremely dangerous, therefore I am not responsible for the possible consequences that could arise from the use of said rituals. There's a reason they're kept strictly secret, only being accessible after a formal initiation process.

But the problem is that to perform these rituals and get results you don't need to be an initiate in the matter. Absolutely anyone can perform them and that is what makes them especially dangerous.

The magic of evocation of spirits is not for beginners. Since an evocation ritual basically consists of bringing a creature that is in another dimension to this world through a portal that opens during the ritual. The problem is that when you call a spirit, they all listen to you. And the spirit that has been called is not always the one that responds to the call.

Evocation rituals are secret formulas to open portals to other dimensions and once a portal is opened any spirit can pass through, even more than one spirit. So how do you know that the spirit that has come to your call is really the spirit that you have conjured up? How do you get rid of an otherworldly creature that is suddenly a threat to your existence?

It is important to know and remember that spirits possess the ability to shape shift, which allows them to seamlessly assume any type of appearance they need, depending on the occasion. And the spirits described in this book master this practice extraordinarily, since they are able to appear adopting the image of the ideal partner of the person who conjures them.

That happens because they know the secrets of the darkest corners of your mind, your tastes and your deepest desires. They play with advantage and almost always win. They show us what they want us to see or what we want to see. And very rarely will we be able to see a spirit as it really is.

A couple of friends in need of quick riches wandered into a forest in Java, Indonesia, accompanied by an *archan* or magician. They stopped in front of the slope of Mount *Semeru*, next to a deep and gloomy cave. The *archan* asked them if they were really sure they wanted to make the pact. One of them backed out at the last moment, but the other said he wished to continue, and the *archan* smeared his eyes with a special ointment and told him to walk into the cave.

Before disappearing into the darkness, the boy who stayed behind could see what looked like a gigantic snake receiving his friend inside the cave. Later, when he left the cave, his friend said that he had found a woman of unimaginable beauty inside.

This is just one example of the power of hypnosis that these spirits have to manipulate their victims, immersing them in a fictional virtual reality that only exists in the victim's mind, which is completely convinced that everything is real.

The spirits in this book can normally be conjured in the sea, rivers, lakes, streams, wells, caves, mountains, forests, deserts, and even in the bathroom of your own home. But it is not that they live in those places literally speaking. Rather, they are portals through which these spirits can more easily and quickly access this physical plane.

This occurs because each of these places accumulates a specific type of energy that makes the manifestation of the appropriate spirit possible. That is to say that the spirits of the water do not physically live in the water. Rather, the water acts as a door through which the spirit enters and leaves this world. That is why those who have a connection to a water spirit sometimes only need a bowl full of water to perform the conjuration.

* * *

Many readers contact me by email requesting my instructions to make a pact with a spirit in exchange for wealth and material goods. They seem very sure of what they want and want to go ahead despite all my warnings. But let me tell you something: calling the devil is not the same as seeing him coming. Whatever situation you may be going through right now, don't forget that sometimes the remedy can be worse than the disease.

When you are desperate or going through serious difficulties, your mind does not think clearly and you would be willing to do anything. At that point you are not only very vulnerable to scammers but you could also fall into the hands of the wrong spirit. Some of those people who contact me would even be willing to sacrifice the life of one or more loved ones in their immediate environment and would do almost anything I told them to.

Now I want to make it clear that I am not trying to judge anyone nor am I entitled to do so, but I am obligated to warn you that whatever you do with your body or with your spirit is completely your business, but you have no moral authority to negotiate with someone else's soul. You will not find rituals that allow you to perform immoral acts in my books, nor will you get any help from me if you write to me requesting such rituals.

I may be an unconventional author, since my main purpose is not to sell my books at all costs. My main goal is to impart knowledge and that means showing you everything, both the good and the bad. As I have already mentioned before, there is a very serious reason why the rituals that appear in my books have been kept secret by the different esoteric traditions.

The information gathered in this work comes mainly from the *vaudou* of the West African coasts, where the spirits of the water are taken very seriously and the experts in those rituals prefer that their knowledge remain secret, being only accessible through a ritual of initiation, accompanied by a long period of training. And all that has to be done for a very important reason.

The main problem is that not everyone has a chance to meet a real guru for a formal initiation, because scammers are everywhere. The false spiritual teachers have become a veritable plague making it practically impossible to tell the difference between the false and the true gurus.

The first batch of scammers is widely distributed all over the internet, especially on the big social platforms like *Facebook* and *Youtube* where they run their scams, taking advantage of people's naivety and desperation. But it's not hard to spot these scammers because almost all of them have the same *modus operandi,* which is to require you to send money to their accounts before beginning your spiritual work.

These scammers will tell you to send them your personal information, such as your name, age, photo, and location, so they can do your work remotely. But anyone with a basic understanding of water spirits knows that no work involving those spirits can be done online or remotely.

It is a strictly personal spiritual work, in which the connection must be made directly between the practitioner and the spirit of the water, without intermediaries. No magician in the world can conjure up a water spirit and send it to another person in another part of the world. The only thing that said magician can do is guiding and giving instructions on how the ritual should be performed.

In order for the magician to help, the person concerned has to be present. Then said magician will act as an intermediary or *medium* between the two parties. He will communicate to the interested party the requirements and conditions that the spirit demands so that the ritual can be carried out. He will also carry out the mystical tasks required to complete the magical work.

The problem lies precisely in finding a truly competent magician, capable of really doing all of the above. Because scammers not only operate online, but unfortunately also scam people in person.

I am aware that it would be impossible for me to fight all that army of physical and electronic scammers, but I am also convinced that ignorance is fought mainly with knowledge and the more people have access to true magic, the less people will continue to be scammed.

But don't forget that knowledge has a price and with all power comes great responsibility. Magic is not a game. Rituals should not be used out of curiosity or to pass the time. When you call a spirit every one of them hears you and it will be difficult for you to know if the spirit you have conjured is the one that has answered the call.

Even after reading my books, people keep emailing me, asking for a much more effective method of conjuring up a spirit that will make them rich and famous faster. Many of these people do not even bother to practice the rituals that I describe in such detail.

They keep asking for a much easier and faster method to get rich, almost instantly. They want the formula to be rich without lifting a finger and offering practically nothing in return. Many of them would not dare to go near a beach or go into the forest in the middle of the night to perform the rituals, because they are full of fear and are easily frightened. But let me tell you that if you are afraid of the dark, of ghosts and especially of snakes, then you should not practice the rituals that are described in this book.

Magic is not for the lazy or timid and definitely nothing is free in the universe. You have to give in order to receive. That is the principle that governs the universe. And in magic, what you give will be proportional to what you receive. So it is not advisable to be greedy, because the more you ask, the more you will have to return.

You can't offer a goat as a sacrifice and expect to get a million dollars in return. That's ridiculous. Money, like everything that exists, is essentially made up of energy. And it takes a huge amount of energy to produce a million dollars. That's why people who make deals with spirits with the sole intention of getting money right away often find themselves in the direst situations.

The spirits do not make money out of thin air, they need a source of energy to produce it and human energy is the most powerful to offer as a sacrifice, since the human being is above all other creatures in this physical dimension.

The only thing more powerful than human blood is the soul itself, which is composed of an immeasurable amount of energy. Spirits love energy because it makes them more powerful, while human beings use money to achieve the same goal. Now imagine asking a spirit that you want to be as rich as Bill Gates or Elon Musk, without having to work as hard as they have. How many souls do you think you would have to sacrifice?

But fortunately for those who make these kinds of greedy deals, the spirits are usually not that demanding when it comes to the soul they are offered. In most cases, they will settle for any soul, as long as it comes from a young and healthy individual.

And there are different methods of getting that kind of innocent souls: one of them may consist of offering a pre-bewitched gift to any person. In reality, what you do is mark that person spiritually so that the spirit with which you have made the pact knows the person who has to be taken away, which usually happens within a period of no more than seven days.

Another method is to place a haunted object somewhere near a road where vehicles frequently travel. After a few days, accidents will begin to occur every time a vehicle travels on that stretch of road. All those killed in these accidents will end up directly in the clutches of the spirit. And the other, more drastic method is to collaborate with said spirit to cause a tsunami, tidal wave, or earthquake in order to collect as many souls as possible at once.

Now it is possible that someone wonders why these spirits do not get those souls on their own, without the need to reach an agreement with a human being. Well, the answer would surprise you. A spirit from the other world needs an authorization to carry out any type of act in this dimension of ours. Some cannot even enter our world without being previously invited either by mentioning their names or performing a ritual to call them.

If that were not the case, imagine the amount of chaos that could be in the world. Western vampires and Asian *Pontilianak* are a very close example, since both beings need express authorization to enter your home. That is one of the many rules of the universe and that all spirits must obey.

But it is important to know that not only creatures from other worlds use a person's soul to obtain power, this practice is also carried out by some human beings. In Taoism there is a spiritualist branch called *Maoshan*.

That branch is dedicated almost exclusively to dealing with the spirits of the deceased, especially the spirits of the recently deceased. One of the most terrible practices of the *Maoshan* adherents is to absorb the soul of the recently deceased like someone absorbing smoke from a cigarette.

It is a ritual that consists of standing on top of the grave of the deceased and pronouncing some mantras several times, until finally a kind of white smoke begins to rise through the grave.

At that moment the individual who is on top of the grave opens his mouth and begins to swallow the smoke, that is actually the soul of the deceased. This ritual is only effective if it is practiced during the first three days of the death of the deceased.

It is said that this practice grants longevity and increases the psychic powers of the individual who performs it. In addition, *Maoshan* adherents carry out another practice that consists of collecting the souls of the recently deceased; to sell them later or to use those for their own twisted purposes.

Some of these souls are kept in jars such as bottles, tied to physical objects such as rings or pendants and also often put in dolls. That is the reason and the origin of so many possessed objects that can be found on places like *eBay*, although most of them are frauds.

As you can see, some rituals are so dark and so terrible that they should never see sunlight. And certainly it is not my intention to describe these rituals here, but I believe that it is a duty for all those who start on the path of dealing with entities from the afterlife to know some basic realities for the good of their own souls. Because it's actually really chilling how easily your soul could be taken from you at any time, without warning, and remains enslaved for an indefinite period, under unimaginable conditions.

But a person's soul or blood are not the only bargaining chips in dealing with spirits. There is also a very powerful element that is sexual energy and that is the third strongest currency that exists in the spiritual world. Although in this book what I recommend using is sexual energy as payment to the spirits in exchange for favors, I must warn that there are also serious risks to the health of the person if this energy is extracted too frequently. This could even cause death.

And I want to make it clear that I am not talking here about the mere physical energy that is lost during sexual intercourse between ordinary humans, but about a much more powerful energy. I speak of the very vital essence of a person. Since the soul is composed of energy, this energy can be extracted from a person during the sexual act, which would be like extracting a piece of his soul, diminishing it and thus weakening the physical body.

And it's not just the water spirits that we'll mention in this book that can extract your life essence during sex; the bad news is that many human beings are capable of it as well. You just have to know the correct procedure to do it. Even tantric sex contains the keys to achieve it. This type of person is part of the group known in spiritualism as energy vampires. And they use any means at their disposal to steal the life essence of their victims and use it for their own ends.

In order to avoid the energetic exhaustion of the people with whom they have relationships, some spirits tend to establish visiting guidelines by mutual agreement between both parties. Some will only come once a week and others usually come twice. But there are also those spirits that do not have any fixed visit schedule established and can appear at any time of the day or night, without prior notice.

And usually all water spirits are extremely jealous and possessive. Just imagine the most possessive and jealous person you've ever met and multiply that by a hundred. But the behavior of those spirits towards you will depend mainly on the agreements established at the time of establishing the pact with them. To obtain more information on this matter, it is necessary to go to the next chapter, where we will talk in detail about these spirits.

ABOUT WATER SPIRITS

Much has been said about the spirits of the water since ancient times. Countless books and articles have been written about them, but all those books have been written by scholars based on stories and legends told in turn by other people, none of whom have ever had contact with any water spirit.

The difference between my books and those of other authors is that their books only talk about the spirits of the water, while mine will put you in direct contact with those spirits. They write about the theoretical part and I focus on the practice.

There is a reason why my books are relatively short. And that's because I skip theory as much as I can to focus directly on practice since I consider that magic is not theoretical. But I also think that it is important for the practitioner to know beforehand the kind of spirit he is about to conjure before carrying out the ritual. So this section will be like a brief introduction to the world of the spirits of the water.

First of all, anyone who intends to perform the rituals in this book must first forget everything that the legends tell about the spirits of the water, commonly known as mermaids. They do not have the tail of a fish nor do they live in castles submerged in the ocean. That stereotype has been so perpetuated through the centuries that it has become part of people's collective unconscious.

In their worlds of origin, the water spirits have the same physiognomy as a human woman and move like them. The only thing that differentiates them from an ordinary woman is that these beings have very pale and glowing skin. Their hair is so long that it practically reaches their feet and their bodies continuously emit an intense exotic and aphrodisiac fragrance that makes them irresistible to men. In addition, their bodies have a strange consistency, as if they were not one hundred percent solid.

Their faces are peaceful and gentle. Their bodies are endowed with voluptuous curves marked out under tight dresses and are covered in jewels and other glittering ornaments from head to toe which gives them a completely exceptional appearance that captivates you from the first moment.

They are very tall women, like supermodels, and they all appear to be under twenty-five years old. But their traits are slightly different, due to many factors. The water spirits found in the Indian Ocean regions have similar features to the inhabitants of those regions. For example, *Ratu Laut Selatan,* who is the Queen of the South Sea and who rules over much of the Indian Ocean, has the appearance of an aristocrat from Java, Indonesia.

Ratu Laut Selatan, as well as *Nyi Blorong, Dewi Lanjar, Dewi Danu* and the rest of the water spirits with whom she shares command of the Indian Ocean, always wears clothing similar to that worn by Indonesian aristocrats in ancient times.

Ratu Laut Selatan, also known as *Kanjeng Ratu Kidul,* is a very powerful and revered queen of the sea throughout the Indian Ocean, where she is given the same cult as other water spirits such as *Yemanja* in the Caribbean countries or *Mami Wata,* in West African countries. She even has a beach named *Parangtritis* on the south coast of Java dedicated in her honor.

Ratu Laut Selatan © Suaramerdeka.id

She also has room number 308 at the *Samudra Beach Hotel,* located in the west of the island of Java, reserved exclusively for her and the interior is fully decorated in her honor. And daily offerings are deposited and prayers are made to ask for the blessings of the queen of the Indian Ocean.

Room 308 of the *Samudra Beach Hotel* © Sutami

Ratu Laut Selatan's favorite color is green and it is the predominant color in her kingdom. It is strictly forbidden to wear clothing of that color to bathe on *Parangtritis* beach, and those who have dared to transgress this rule have suffered reprisals from *Ratu Laut Selatan*.

On the other hand, the water spirits that reign in the Atlantic Ocean, particularly on the coasts of West Africa, have traits similar to those of Hindu women or Southeast Asian women. Specifically, Indonesia, Thailand and Cambodia and sometimes they wear traditional clothes of the former aristocrats of those countries. They look nothing like

African women even though there are paintings depicting them with black skin, but in fact they actually have very pale skin, as already mentioned.

Typical appearance of a water spirit © Benito Torres

Those water spirits are known in that part of the African continent as *Mami Wata* and their favorite color is white. That is the color that predominates in the cities where these beings live. The buildings, the streets, the clothes and even the gardens are white, full of white flowers. For this reason, they require all their followers to use the color white, both when performing rituals and in their daily lives.

The name *Mami Wata* refers to all the spirits of the water and not to a particular spirit. In fact, not all of those spirits come from the same dimension or reside in the same realm. Even those who come from the same place can have completely different personalities. Just like with humans.

It should be noted that the spirits called *Mami Wata* are not only worshiped in West Africa, but have become a true international phenomenon and are currently revered and recognized in more than twenty countries around the world. So influential are these spirits that they have become an official religion in several countries. Among them are Togo, Nigeria and Benin, which are considered to be the cradle of the *Mami Wata* cult.

People from different parts of the world come to West Africa to receive the *Mami Wata* initiation, as well as to perform rituals for wealth and prosperity which generally require a marriage, a pact or an alliance with those spirits of the water as a requirement to receive their blessing.

Initiation ritual to *Mami Wata* © Benito Torres

It is important to note that the fact that I refer to these beings as *spirits* does not mean that they are incorporeal entities like ghosts. In reality they have physical and tangible bodies like human beings. And the cities where they reside are as real as ours. These are not spiritual cities located on the astral plane or submerged under water.

They are physical cities with tangible people and buildings. The only difference is that all of that is on a different plane of existence than humans. But you can travel to those cities both physically and spiritually. The secret is to know the key to make such trips.

Normally a full day in the world of water spirits is equivalent to many days in the world of humans. That is why it is safer to travel to that world in a spiritual way rather than in a physical way. Because when you are there in a spiritual way, the time of that world is synchronized with ours. But the same does not happen when you make the trip physically.

To travel to the world of the water spirits in a spiritual way, it is not necessary to go near the sea or a river. It is enough to fall asleep or plunge into a kind of trance and the astral body will make the trip. On the other hand, to make the trip in a physical way, you have to move to a water source large and deep enough to be completely submerged and immediately you reach the other world.

Another interesting fact to keep in mind is that in the world of water spirits, most of the population is female. Perhaps it is because water is an element of a purely feminine nature. In any case, several trips to that world can be made without ever meeting any male.

In the kingdom of water everything is love and happiness. You can see women laughing and talking to each other, others dance and sing, some are swimming in ponds and others are dedicated to combing their long hair. A sense of peace and joy is felt all around. It's like being in paradise. The world of humans pales in comparison to that of the water spirits. As if the world of those spirits was of a higher definition than that of humans.

Everything shines brighter and you experience the feeling of being more alive and freer. As if you had lived until that moment being locked in a bottle. For that reason, very few people want to return to the human world. But there is a risk that if you spend too much times in the spirit world you could pass away in the physical world.

Water transmits peace, calm and tranquility. Everyone experiences a feeling of euphoria by the sea, next to a lake or a river. Even the simple sound of the rain falling on the roof or beating against the window makes us so calm that sometimes we fall asleep.

The water spirits are some of the best a person can come across in the spirit world. Water women are extremely affectionate with their human husbands. They love passionately and can't stand when their husband is romantically involved with other woman which makes them seem quite possessive.

They are overprotective and take care of their human husbands twenty-four hours a day, both spiritually and physically, keeping him away from visible and invisible dangers. And they will immediately attack anyone who tries to cause harm to their charges.

Such is the love of a water woman towards her husband that she dedicates her entire existence to him and solves all his material and spiritual needs. She knows everything he wants, even without him having to say it. Because she can read your thoughts and feel your emotions as if they were her own.

The mere presence of the water spirit transmits peace and calm to her husband, eliminating all his pain, stress and anxiety. They are able to eliminate suffering and put out a person's anger or inner fire, just as water puts out the flames of a bonfire.

And contrary to what some people tend to think, the water spirits are not evil in nature, considering the passive nature of the water element in general and the purifying properties of the sea in particular. So the fear of these people towards the spirits of the water is completely absurd and has its origin in ignorance.

First you have to remember that there is a barrier between the world of humans and the world of spirits. And now it must be understood that practically no spirit has the interest to initiate contact with the human species, among other things because they consider us an underdeveloped, mediocre and materialistic species.

Humans are the ones who always transgress the laws of the universe, crossing the barrier between worlds and opening portals through rituals and other techniques in order to come into contact with spirits and creatures from other dimensions all this for petty and materialistic purposes. Making promises to beings from other worlds to make their worldly wishes come true and then breaking those promises.

Everywhere there is talk of demonic possessions, of people harassed by succubi or incubi, of sexual relations in dreams and other similar things. But few people have the curiosity to wonder why specific individuals seem to have been chosen by the spirits that haunt them. Why can two people sleep in the same bed and only one of them is continually harassed by the spirit while the other person is completely left out?

That's because these spirits don't attack people randomly. The origin of the problem usually resides in the past of the person who is being attacked, an act that he performed in this life or in one of his previous lives. The causes can be so numerous that it would be impossible for me to list them all in this book.

Some of the most common reasons usually consist of a ritual that the individual performed. Sometimes people make pacts with a water spirit and then break the pact agreements and think they got away with it. What these people don't know is that the spirits are very patient because they have all the time in the world and they will haunt you in your next lives.

Other times marriages are performed with spirits of water or other dimensions, thinking that the relationship would come to an end upon death. But it turns out that the spirit decides to accompany the person in his next live and continue to be his spiritual spouse. Being able to destroy any type of serious sentimental relationship that said person wanted to maintain.

The cause of the problem can also reside in an act that the person performed, involuntarily causing the reaction of the water spirits. For example: piss, spit, defecate or perform sexual intercourse in water. Sometimes even having sex with a person who has a connection to the water spirits can cause those spirits to have access to you as well.

Those are some of the ways that the spirits of the water can enter your life. But as I already said before, the list is quite long. But in all cases it can be verified that the human being is the one who opens the doors of his life to the spirit, either voluntarily or involuntarily. At no time do these spirits attempt to initiate contact with us first.

There is a list of common clues that can signal the presence of a water spirit in your life, even if you don't know it. Some of those signs are as follows:

a) Very vivid and recurring erotic dreams.

b) Continuously hearing a mysterious woman's voice calling you by your name.

c) The sudden and recurring smell of a mysterious and exotic perfume.

d) Having sexual relations while awake or semi-asleep with unknown or invisible women.

e) Dreaming that you are frequently swimming in the sea or in the river and that you can breathe underwater.

f) Frequently dreaming that you are in the company of snakes or crocodiles.

It's funny to see pastors and evangelists everywhere claiming to have powers to drive out the water spirits, at the same time that some parishioners of these congregations claim to be possessed by said spirits, what is in fact a hoax.

To understand what I am saying you only have to take a look at the endless list of books available online written by these shepherds, each one of them claiming to have the ultimate key to rid people of the spirits of the water. A simple search in any online bookstore will return dozens of books in that category.

The funny thing is that these pastors and evangelists have no real knowledge about the spirits they claim to combat. They do not have any real information about them, apart from the stories they hear and the data they find in the books. In fact, the main reference for these people is the Bible, whose verses they use to compose their fraudulent books, without providing any original information.

The supposed fight against the spirits of the water is actually a business well set up by these unscrupulous individuals, who deliberately sow fear among their parishioners so that they can later sell their books and profit in this way at their expense. After all, isn't that what the church has always done to survive?

On the other hand, the spirits of the water do not possess people spiritually. All they do is influence people in a psychic way, being able to change their habits or they can show you spectral and terrifying visions, when their intention is to scare you. Therefore the people who claim to be possessed by these spirits are deceivers or are simply dealing with some other type of entity.

Most of these people are not usually questioned or questioned about the possible origin of their spiritual attacks. What acts could they have performed in the past? But when questioned and they decide to tell the truth, their testimonies are often chilling. So it is understood that the spiritual attacks of the water spirits do not occur randomly at all.

There is so much ignorance and confusion regarding the water spirits and many people talk and write about them without even bothering to know about them which creates more confusion among the masses. But the problem is precisely in the term *water spirits* that people habitually use to refer to all spiritual beings that come from water.

Now it has to be understood that there is absolutely no spirit living in the water, as I have already mentioned earlier in this book. Water is simply a portal that many types of spirits use to enter and exit this dimension of ours and those are known as *water spirits.*

This is perfectly understood the first time a dimensional journey is made using the water element to access other dimensions. Because when you arrive on the other side you discover that your clothes are completely dry, despite the fact that you crossed the water on the journey. And the same thing happens when you come back. Then you discover that there is no such thing as the world of water, but rather the illusion of submerging yourself in water.

In the same way the elementals of the earth do not live inside the earth. The fire elementals do not live inside the flames nor do the air elementals live in the air. They are simply portals through which they manifest. There are truths that cannot be understood with the mind and to understand them we must first evolve.

But one thing is quite clear in this matter. Anything that a spirit uses to manifest itself seems to greatly influence that spirit's qualities, as well as its personality. That is why the spirits of the four elements seem to possess completely different characteristics from each other.

There is a multitude of spirits that use the water element, from those belonging to high hierarchies such as *Devas* and *Devis* , including *Apsaras, Yakshinis, Yoginis, Naginis* and *Bhootinis,* to beings belonging to the lower astral such as the spirits of drowned people and others lower creatures.

For this reason, when an evocation ritual is performed for beings of the water element, there is a high probability that a creature from the lower astral plane will attend, posing as the evoked spirit. And most of the negative experiences that are recorded when performing these types of rituals are usually due to these kinds of impostor spirits.

It is also important to always know and remember that the types and categories of spirits that come to the evocations generally depend on the state of consciousness and the level of spiritual evolution of the person performing the evocation.

The state of consciousness plays a crucial role in magic in general and in the evocation of spirits in particular. For example, a person dominated by lust, hate, and other negative emotions is expected to attract only spirits who share those kinds of emotions.

In the same way, a person with a low level of spiritual evolution and without any mastery in the evocation of spirits cannot expect a higher being of the *Deva* category to come to his evocation, simply because his *Chi* is not powerful enough to conjure these superior spirits.

And it is also advisable to always start with the softer and lower rituals, when starting to practice a new system of magic and gradually continue to climb to the top. And whenever possible you should first go through an initiation ritual.

There are infinite esoteric traditions devoted solely to the worship of the spirits of water. They are spread all over the planet and the procedures and rituals they use to establish contact with these spirits are very varied depending on the culture and geographical location.

Some of these rituals are very complex and require several days to perform, including the recitation of thousands of mantras daily. As is the case with the conjuration of *Kanjeng Ratu Kidul*, the queen of the Indian Ocean, who belongs to a category of superior spirits.

However, other rituals are relatively simpler, such as the evocation of *Dewi Lanjar*, who rules the north coast of Java, Indonesia. Whose ritual consists of reciting *Surah Al-Ikhlas* for 41 times and then the person has to sleep at the front door of his home.

Dewi Lanjar, ruler of the north coast of Java.

People from Java often perform the *Dewi Lanjar* ritual to gain fortune and riches but the price to pay is the life of the person who performs the ritual or that of one of their closest relatives. It is a well-known ritual in Indonesia and is frequently performed due to its extreme simplicity.

Another way to make quick money in Indonesia is through the pact or *pesugihan* with *Nyi Blorong,* who is second in command in the kingdom of *Kanjeng*

Ratu Kidul. *Nyi Blorong* is a spirit belonging to the group of *Naginis*, creatures with the bust of a woman and the lower part in the form of a snake. In fact, it is said that her true form is that of a huge green snake.

But she never appears in her original *Nagini* form, but as a woman endowed with unearthly beauty, her body covered in shimmering and exquisite ornaments of gold and precious stones.

Nyi Blorong © Celvinisasi

Or at least that is the image described by those who have been in the presence of that water spirit. It may not be her authentic appearance, taking into account that the spirits can modify the perception we have of them.

A man from Java, Indonesia had a pact with a *Nagini* and she visited him every Friday evening. The man had a special room where he received visits from the spirit and where no one else ever entered.

The only problem was that said man had a wife and she also lived in that house. The man slept every night with that human wife in the matrimonial room, but every Friday he went into the room where no one else entered to meet his spirit woman and did not come out until the next day.

His wife was intrigued and the man never offered her any satisfactory explanation as to why he locked himself in that mysterious room every Friday. One night the woman decided to find out the truth and peeked through a crack next to the lock on the door of that room, where her husband had locked himself up again as usual. It was a very tiny crack but it served so that the woman could glimpse what was happening on the other side of the door.

But what she saw chilled her blood in her veins. She saw her husband in bed with a giant snake lying next to him. A scream escaped from her mouth. She couldn't help it. The next morning her husband did not leave the mysterious room as usual.

He also did not respond to his wife's calls. When the door was finally broken down she found her husband lying dead on the bed. There was no trace of any other person in the room.

That's another example of how a spirit's hypnotic power can alter a person's visual perception. And the *Naginis* perfectly master that technique. In addition, they are in charge of guarding the hidden treasures of the earth and are capable of turning a person immensely rich overnight.

So individuals who make pacts with *Nyi Blorong* become extremely wealthy, for when she returns to her world just before dawn, she often leaves behind all her jewelry and ornaments. Then those objects are sold in the market for large amounts of money.

There are many more spirits like these around the world and also different rituals to get in touch with them. But the rituals I offer in this book are uniquely African and come from adherents of the water spirit cult known as *Mami Wata*. And as the rules indicate, we have to start with the initiation ritual first.

INITIATION TO THE WATER SPIRITS

One who wants to truly establish a connection with the *Mami Wata spirits* must first erect an altar to honor those spirits. The altar serves as a communication portal between the adept and the spirit, a place where the adept makes his requests and deposits his offerings.

Mami Wata altar © Tang Teaching Museum

Said altar can be elaborate or simple. The only important thing is that it consists of the following basic elements: an image or statue of *Mami Wata* or *Yemaya,* a bouquet of flowers, some white candles, a bottle of *Bint El Sudan* talcum powder and a bottle of perfume called *Mami Water*. There should also be a white porcelain plate with fresh fruits, cookies and candies. The presence of a few conches or sea shells is equally important.

Perfume *Mami Water* © Your Super Shop

Mami Wata rituals are recommended to be performed on Friday, during the full moon. The moon acts as an amplifier of the power of the water spirits, as well as other beings from the spirit world. So the practitioner must wait for a Friday that coincides with the full moon to perform any of the *Mami Wata* rituals in this book. Seven days of purification must also be carried out obligatorily before performing the ritual.

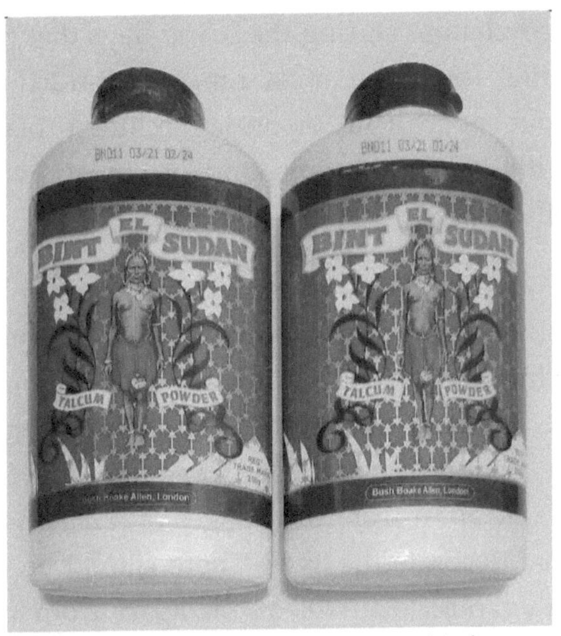

Talc *Bint El Sudan* © Africa Heritage Market

So when you are ready to perform the initiation ritual you first have to start the purification period of seven days, starting from Saturday, to perform the ritual on next week Friday. During that period you must maintain a sattvik diet.

That means your diet has to be completely vegetarian and you should avoid eggs, garlic and onion.

You also have to avoid alcohol, tobacco and any type of sex, including self-stimulation. During the seven days that the ritual lasts, you must remain secluded in your apartment or in a secluded place without making any kind of contact with other people.

The room where the initiation ritual takes place should be completely painted white. If the floor is not white then it should be covered with a white rug. There should be no photographs or decorations on the walls, apart from the images of *Mami Wata* that decorate the altar. There should be no other objects in the room apart from the objects of the altar and a mattress covered with a white sheet that you will use to sleep on. You should not sleep anywhere else during the rituals of *Mami Wata*.

From the beginning of the purification period you must cover your body only with a white ceremonial robe, like the people seen in a picture from this book performing the initiation ritual. No underwear of any kind should be worn under that white robe. And if you are a man you must completely cut your hair.

To carry out the daily purification bath you have to fill a bucket with salt water. That is to say that you have to pour salt into the water in the bucket to purify it. And you should also mix said water with hyssop plants and pour a little of the *Mami Water* perfume. The salt and the hyssop plant have purifying properties and will help you cleanse your aura.

Open a can of skimmed milk and spray your entire body with it. Then wash your body with the water from the bucket. Let the body dry on its own, without using any towels. Then spray your entire body with talcum powder from *Mami Wata's* altar. Also spray the entire room where you are performing the ritual with a little of that talcum powder and a little of the *Mami Water* perfume. The room should be lit only with candles.

Before going to bed you should kneel in front of the altar of *Mami Wata* and express your wishes in detail in a brief, concise and direct way. Why do you want to contact her? What do you want her to do for you? You have to speak with respect and devotion. And above all you must address her as Goddess of the Sea, mother of all waters, since *Mami Wata* means "Mother of Water". This act should be performed both when going to bed and when waking up. Your devotion to the goddess must be absolute.

You also have to shower in the morning and in the afternoon only with the salt water mixed with hyssop plants during the whole course of the initiation ritual, avoiding any kind of cosmetics. The TV has to be kept off and the phones have to be on silent mode. They should not be used to communicate with anyone outside.

On the third day of the ritual you must gather five types of fruits on a white plate. There should also be a bouquet of flowers, candies and cookies as well as a comb and a hand mirror for women. You must meet with these things on the edge of a beach or on the banks of a river, at twelve o'clock at night. Light a candle and stick it to the shore. Then wade ankle-deep in the water and say the following words aloud:

I (your full name), son -or daughter- of (full name of your mother) and (full name of your father) of the family (name of your lineage) residing in (country, city and street name). I come tonight to beg you, oh Goddess of the Sea (express your wish).

After reciting those words, if you find yourself doing the ritual in the sea, you should take advantage of the moment when a wave is returning to the sea to quickly throw your offering. In this way, when said wave leave it will also drag your offering towards the sea. If you are performing the ritual in a river then you simply have to deposit the offering under the water and return home without looking back. Leave the candle burning.

Now you must continue three more days of isolation until the ritual is completed. It is important to write down all the dreams you have during that initiation ritual, without omitting any detail. If you have performed the ritual correctly, *Mami Wata* will contact you through dreams.

This first stage is the most important for anyone who wants to work closely with the spirits of *Mami Wata*. Only after having carried out that stage obtaining success can the rituals indicated in the following chapters be performed.

MARRIAGE WITH A WATER SPIRIT

As its name suggests, this is one of the rituals used to marry *Mami Wata*. Marriage with a water spirit is one of the most powerful rituals in the world. People from all parts of the earth have used these rituals since ancient times to acquire power, wealth or psychic abilities and they are still used today even more than in the past, whether you believe it or not.

There are three options for forming an alliance with a *Mami Wata* spirit: being a devotee of the spirit, being its priest or priestess, being its lover, being its husband or its wife. The last option is the most powerful of all but it also happens to be the most dangerous.

As will be seen in the following pages, the marriage with *Mami Wata* is a purely mystical act and also implies a long list of rules or conditions that must be accepted. One of those conditions usually consists of sharing the rest of your life with a boa or a giant python, which usually resides in the same room as the practitioner and where no one else should enter under any circumstance.

Spirit Serpent in South Africa © Zodwa Wabantu

This is a snake of a purely spiritual nature, more like a totem or a familiar spirit. That snake is the spiritual partner of the practitioner and he or she is obliged to feed it, as well as to make the offerings and sacrifices previously agreed with that snake. If some of the offerings or sacrifices are not made on the established dates, the retaliation of the serpent can be terrifying.

Such rituals are known as *Ukuthwala* in South Africa, where they are frequently practiced by people in need of quick money. Generally these spirit snakes are kept under strict secrecy, but there are people who for unknown reasons tend to display theirs in public.

This type of snake is known as Mamlambo in South Africa and to obtain it you have to go to a Shangoma or sorcerer. That spirit is not associated with the sea but rather with sources of fresh water and it's one of the most difficult creatures to get rid of, because even after the person it made the pact with has died, sometimes the spirit remains to haunt the family members for generations.

But only the dark rituals performed by black magicians attract this type of snakes and other creatures from the lower astral. The fact is that most people prefer this type of ritual because the chances of success are much higher, compared to the evocation of the spirits of the water that reside in higher planes of existence.

Spirits from the lower dimensions come more quickly to evocations because they have a burning thirst for blood, power and energy and they see in human beings the perfect tools to achieve their ambitions.

Higher class water spirits, on the other hand, take more time to introduce themselves. Because first they have to make sure that the person who performs the conjuration is really worth it and lives up to expectations. In that sense they are more demanding than the spirits of the low dimensions.

But when they decide to answer the call, they present themselves as women of angelic beauty. They are full of beauty both inside and out and their bodies seem to glow with a kind of light that comes from within. They are authentic beings of light, whose mere presence makes worries disappear.

Having one of those spirits as your wife is like being married to an angel, they take care of you, they protect you, they grant you success in all your endeavors, they take care of your financial needs, and they even feed you food that is not from this world. And the most important thing is that they are always by your side whenever you need them. They are every man's dream come true.

But these angelic women also have their dark side and it is not recommended to confuse their sweetness with weakness or their indulgence with naivety. Because they are capable of destroying a person without warning, with astonishing speed and ease, if that person breaks any of their agreements. They can strip you of all your wealth and turn you into a beggar.

Because these spirits usually establish their own conditions and one of them is absolute fidelity. The practitioner must avoid any type of sentimental or sexual relationship with any other woman. Because the *Mami Wata* spirits are extremely jealous and can sometimes seem possessive. So a practitioner who doesn't have children yet may never be able to have offspring.

Apart from absolute loyalty and fidelity, the practitioner may also be forced to modify a large part of his habitual customs. He could leave alcohol, tobacco and other toxic substances. He could also be forced to stop consuming certain foods, frequenting certain places, and associating with certain people.

He may also be forced to dress in a certain way, using clothing of a specific color. In the same way, the practitioner could commit to making certain types of offerings or sacrifices from time to time, in honor of his spiritual woman of water.

Now it is important to warn that from the moment you perform an alliance or marriage ritual with the spirits of this book you will not be able to back out again. Your soul will be linked to these spirits and you will have to assume the advantages and disadvantages that this union supposes. The influence of these spirits will manifest in you physically or spiritually, directly or indirectly.

Even when it seems to you that the ritual did not work, the reality may turn out to be completely different. Spirits react differently to humans and are completely unpredictable. A spirit can be with you throughout your life, making no effort to reveal its presence to you, but projecting its influence on you.

If it is a spiritual husband or wife, then it will be in charge of destroying all the serious sentimental relationships that you want to maintain. It will cause you depression, anxiety and self-destructive behaviors. And it will only stop when you find a way to appease it or until you correctly carry out a ritual that you started but couldn't finish in the right way.

* * *

Now that you have a slight idea of what marriage with *Mami Wata* entails, all that remains is to gather the following material to perform the ritual:

1. Four white candles
2. Three parrot feathers
3. Eight freshly laid chicken eggs
4. A completely white rooster
5. A completely white duck
6. A white basket
7. *Mami Water* perfume
8. A hollowed out gourd
9. Incense sticks

10. *Bint El Sudan* talcum powder
11. A hand mirror for women
12. Twelve sea cowries
13. Different jewelry for women
14. Four units of five types of fruit (Example: four mangoes, four apples, four bananas, etc.)
15. Skimmed milk
16. A black thread
17. Two pieces of white cloth
18. A knife.
19. A rosary of 108 white beads.

Cowry shells © Rudraksha Ratna

When you have gathered this list of items and are ready to begin the ritual, then you should wait for the month in which the full moon falls on a Friday. Then you will have to carry out the seven days of purification, maintaining a sattvik diet, avoiding the pleasures of the flesh and avoiding communication with the rest of the people, as indicated in the initiation ritual previously mentioned in this book.

On Friday at sunset you have to write on a white sheet with a blue pen exactly what you want to get from the water spirits. You can use the following example for inspiration:

I (your full name), son -or daughter- of (full name of your mother) and (full name of your father) of the family (name of your lineage) residing in (country, city and street name). I come tonight to beg you, oh Great Yemanja, Goddess of the Sea, that you grant me the hand of one of your daughters, so that I can take her as a wife and may she bring me wealth and prosperity until the day I die.

After writing that letter you must sign three times below. Then you have to prick the little finger of your left hand with

a pin and let a few drops of your blood fall
on the paper, just below your last signature.

At twelve o'clock that same night
you must head toward the edge of the sea
or a river with all the objects indicated on
the list, after performing the daily ritual
bath. You must be dressed in the traditional
white garment, which consists basically of a
white cloth wrapped around your body.

Hollowed out gourd © Percusión Africana

After depositing all the objects on the
shore, you have to undress and pour the
talcum powder all over your skin, starting
from the head to the feet. Then get dressed
again and spray your body with *Mami
Water* perfume. Now you have to cover the
bottom of the white basket with one of the

two white fabrics. He begins to deposit the five kinds of fruit inside the white basket. Also deposit the mirror, the women's jewelry next to the fruits, as well as the skimmed milk.

Now you must go to the very edge of the water with the duck, the knife and the white basket. After placing the basket next to you, you have to open the skimmed milk, take a drink and you spit it out in the water then the skimmed milk is putted back in the basket. You must then hold the duck with both hands in front of you while reciting the following words:

Oh Great Yemaya Goddess of the sea.
Open the doors of the world of water in order for
one of your daughters to come to me to be with
me as my wife and may she bring me wealth and
prosperity.
Until the day I die.

After repeating those words for three times, you should recite the following mantra for twelve times:

Maanstrofanz |
Maanstonantuum |

Maanzristrofranduum |
Mandestonans | [1]

After that you should say:

Oh Great Yemaya, accept this offering that I
bring you this day.
Open the portal to the world of water

Then you have to slaughter the duck using the knife, making the blood spill first on your feet (without letting it stain your dress) and then on the water. Then make the blood drip back onto your legs and immediately afterwards make it drip back onto the water, back and forth. This act must be performed three times.

Then the duck's blood must be dripped onto the basket containing the offerings. The blood should be spilled in a circle, in a clockwise direction. Then the head of the duck must be completely cut off and placed on top of the offerings in the basket. Then the basket is held with both hands and stretched forwards and then backwards. Then it goes back and forth.

---

[1] Mantra 01

This act is also performed three times, the same as with the duck's blood, in a back-and-forth manner. On the third time that you lean forward, you must say the following words three times:

After that you must go knee-deep in the water and deposit the basket. Then you return to the shore walking backwards, without turning your back to the water. After reaching the shore you have to draw a circle on the ground with the talcum powder, in a clockwise direction. Place four candles in the four cardinal directions, along with four incense sticks.

Now you have to spread the second white cloth in the center of the circle and place the pumpkin on top. Then you have to deposit the letter you wrote inside the pumpkin. Then you take seven of the eight eggs you brought and place them on top of the card. Then you have to spread a little *Bint El Sudan* talcum powder on top of the eggs and the letter. You take two parrot feathers and place them on top of the eggs and spread the talc again.

Now place the twelve shells on the other objects in the pumpkin and sprinkle some talcum powder again and also pour a little of the *Mami Water* perfume on the objects in the pumpkin, in a clockwise direction.

Then you should light the four candles placed in the four directions, like the incense, in a clockwise direction. Then you have to take the white chicken and raise it by presenting it first to the north sail, then to the south, east and west. Then you stand facing the water and present the rooster up and then down.

Now raise the rooster high again and pronounce the following words:

> *Ehuu, Ehuu, Ehuu*
> (You pause)
> *Ehuu, Ehuu, Ehuu*
> (You pause again)

Ehuu, Ehuu, Ehuu |[2]

Oh Great Yemaya Goddess of the sea.
Open the doors of the world of water in order for
one of your daughters to come to me to be with
me as my wife and may she bring me wealth and
prosperity until the day I die. | |

Oh Divine Mother.
Through the blood of that animal that has been
shed,
I establish my alliance with you.
I establish my alliance with the world of water.
I establish my alliance with the spirits of the
water.
May they come to me and bring me wealth and
prosperity until the day I die.

After reciting those words you have to slaughter the chicken and let some blood spill inside the gourd. Immediately afterwards, you have to go around the circle clockwise, making the chicken's blood fall on the flour that forms the circle, avoiding the candles being extinguished.

---

[2] Mantra 02

The head of the chicken is then cut off and placed inside the gourd. The third feather of the parrot is grasped and extended towards the water, and then the hand is contracted. It extends back towards the water and the hand contracts again. This must be done three times. The feather is then placed in the hole above the ear. Women should place it in their hair, inserting it between the hairs.

Now the last egg must be tied with the black thread so that it does not come loose when it is introduced in the water, also taking care not to break it in the process. Then you must advance to the water and submerge up to your knees, with the egg and the pumpkin in your hands. The gourd is placed in the water and the egg is carefully placed at the bottom of the water.

Then you return to shore by walking backwards again, without turning your back to the water, while carefully unwinding the line to the center of the circle. So the black thread to which the egg is tied must be long enough to cover several meters in length. And it must also be thick enough not to break.

White rosary of 108 beads © Beads Portal

Upon entering the circle you must sit on the white cloth facing the water and tie the black thread on the little finger of your left hand. Then you must recite the following mantra for 108 times using the white rosary. This means that you have to complete a complete round of the rosary:

Extrantuum Krantuum Frantuum | [3]

If you have performed the ritual correctly, before you complete the recitation

---

[3] Mantra 03

of the mantras something will happen. Because spirits are unpredictable, I can't tell you for sure what will come out of the water. That will depend on several factors, including your own karma. But whatever you see you must face it with courage.

At the end of the ritual you must untie the black thread from your finger, walk backwards out of the circle and leave the place without looking back, taking with you the white rosary and the parrot feather. That night and for the next three nights you must sleep in the ritual room.

PACT WITH THE GODDESS *DEMARASHAGI*

The goddess *Demarashagi* is one of the many goddesses who rule the ocean. She is a goddess little known to the uninitiated and her rituals are also kept secret. She is one of those who have the keys to *Pandemonium* and guardian of all its treasures. This goddess is capable of granting great wealth to people who make alliances or pacts with her.

Now, it is important to point out that there is a difference between the alliance, the marriage and the pact with the spirits. This is a subtle difference, but a very important one. For example, a friendship between a human and a spirit or the connection between a faithful and a deity can be interpreted as an alliance.

When a human and a spirit establish a sentimental relationship as formal spouses, previously setting prerequisites for mutual coexistence, then this can be considered as a marriage.

Instead a pact is only a commercial exchange between the human and the spirit or deity. The spirit grants the human a wish or offers a service and in return the human gives an offering or sacrifice. That is what is considered a pact in the world of magic.

There are short-term and long-term pacts or agreements. In short-term pacts, once the commercial exchange between the human and the spirit has been carried out, then the pact can be concluded. But in long-term pacts, the spirit agrees to provide its services to the human for a longer period of time, as long as the human continues to offer the agreed sacrifices in return.

The nature of the offerings or sacrifices that the human offers to the spirit will depend mainly on the type of services offered. It is to be expected that a very arduous service will require a proportionate offering. You can't ask a spirit to make you the best singer in the world and expect it to ask you to only sacrifice a sheep in return.

The spirits always demand a sacrifice proportional to the service rendered. The type of sacrifice is established at the time of the pact and must be delivered before or after the human has received the service agreed with the spirit. The sacrifice must always be offered on the established dates. Exactly on the agreed day and time.

It is very important to fulfill all the agreements with the spirits to the letter because they are extremely demanding with the details. They never accept excuses and never forgive mistakes. In addition, agreements cannot be broken once formalized. They can only conclude when both parties have obtained their fair share.

And the spirits always get what is theirs. Because they cannot be deceived nor can they be scammed. You can't run away from them either. Rituals and other tricks can be used to form a kind of protective barrier between the subject and such spirits. But all those remedies are only temporary.

The spirits are patient because they have all the time in the world. If you try to run away from them while you are alive, when you finally die you will find them waiting for you. They are also capable of tormenting you in your future reincarnations. That is why there are people harassed by spirits from the day they were born and many of these people do not even understand why.

Now that you have a slight idea about the pact with the spirits, you only need to get the items from the following list to make the pact with *Mami Wata:*

1. A bottle of *Mami Water perfume.*
2. A bottle of *Bint El Sudan talc.*
3. A white ceremonial suit.
4. A bottle of skimmed milk.
5. Three coconuts.

This ritual, like the rest of the *Mami Wata rituals,* must be performed during the full moon. Therefore the practitioner will begin a five-day fast, which will begin on Monday and end on Friday, which will be the day of the ritual.

During the days of fasting, the practitioner must also follow a sattvic diet, avoiding vices and sensual pleasures, as well as the company of other people and doing everything that has already been previously mentioned during the initiation ritual.

On Friday night, before going to the place of the ritual, you must fill a white bucket with water and pour the content of the three coconuts and a little coarse salt into that water. At midnight the practitioner must be on a beach, a river or a lake to begin the ritual.

The practitioner must be dressed in his white suit and provided with the other objects necessary for the ritual. The first thing to do is spray all over your body with *Mami Water* perfume. If it is a man, you should begin to perfume from head to toe. But if it is a woman then you should start spraying the perfume from the feet to the head.

After that two concentric circles should be traced near the water with *Bint El Sudan* talcum powder. The circles should be large enough so that the practitioner has enough space to perform the ritual inside in comfort.

The skimmed milk bottle should now be opened and spit once into it. After that you must see yourself or throw some milk into the water and put the bottle back on the ground. Then the following symbol must be formed with the right hand.

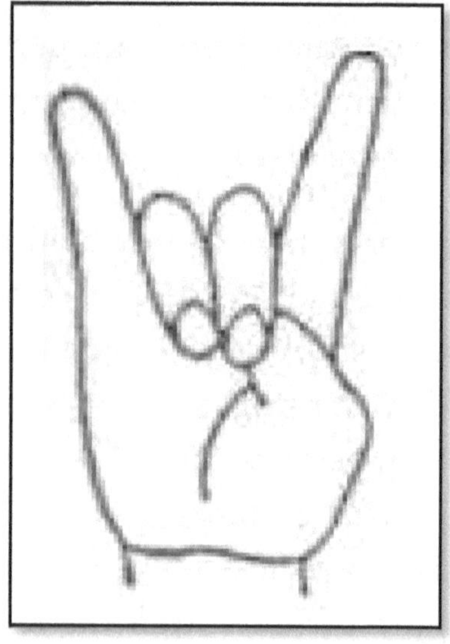

© Paper Blog

While you form this symbol with your hand you must look towards the water and recite the following words three times:

Zubitaa.
Eweemayaa.
Zubaa-Zubaa.
Amasunde.
Rebete-Kete.
Zubaa-Zubaa | [4]

O great Demarashagi Great Goddess of Water.
Open the doors of space and time for me in the
name of the Pentagramaton and the
Tetagrammaton.
By the power of Almighty God the one who said
let there be light and there was light.
Open the doors of Pandemonium for me so that
all the treasures and all the riches of this world
are mine. | |

Zubitaa.
Ewemayaa.
Zubaa-Zubaa.
Amasunde.
Rebete
Zubaa-Zubaa | |

After pronouncing those words three times, if you have pronounced them correctly then the milk bottle will start to

---

[4] Mantra 04

vibrate slightly. As if she was possessed by an invisible force. The practitioner must remain immobile looking towards the water, without ever leaving the circle.

Whatever happens or whatever comes out of the water, the practitioner must never leave the circle. The negotiations or conversations that the practitioner maintains with the spirit must be maintained without leaving the circle at any time. Only when everything is finished should you walk out of the circle in reverse and leave the place.

If fifteen minutes after pronouncing the words of the incantation three times no strange manifestation is observed, the practitioner must also leave the circle, walking backwards and returning home. You must sleep in the ritual room for the next three days.

PACT WITH THE GODDESS *YEMAYA*

Yemaya is one of the main *Orishas* of the religion known as *Santeria,* which is practiced in Latin American countries and also in the Caribbean countries. But the cult of this goddess began mainly in the coastal tribes of Nigeria, in West Africa.

Yemaya, goddess of the sea

This spirit is part of the kingdom of the *Devas* or gods, which is the highest among the six kingdoms that make up

Samsara, so it is endowed with immense power. *Yemaya* has more power and is above other water spirits such as *Ratu Laut Selatan,* who have not yet evolved to the category of *Devas.*

Yemaya is currently better known and revered in the countries of the African Diasporas, while in the African continent what prevails is the cult of *Mami Wata.* Although many claim there is no difference between the two spirits. In fact, *Yemaya* is a manifestation of *Mami Wata,* being herself a spirit from the water.

In this ritual, the practitioner does not make the pact directly with the goddess of water, but rather with one of her innumerable daughters. But as a general rule in magic, to evoke a spirit it is best to ask for the intercession of the ruler of said spirit. In this way the chances of success of the ritual increase considerably.

In this case, the practitioner requests the permission of the goddess *Yemaya* to marry one of her daughters, as also occurs in the marriage ritual with a water spirit described in this book. To perform this ritual you will need the following items:

1. Six white candles.
2. Six red candles.
3. Two silver rings.
4. A white ceremonial robe.
5. A white scarf.
6. Four units of four types of fruit.
7. A hollowed-out pumpkin.
8. *Mommy Water* Perfume.
9. *Bint El Sudan* talc powder.
10. Four coconuts.
11. Four bottles of gin.
12. Four bottles of soft drinks.
13. One hundred grams of rice.
14. A clay pot.
15. Nine kola nuts.

After obtaining all these objects, now they have to fast for seven days accompanied by a sattvik diet and following all the other rules that are respected during the purification process. The best time to start this purification is seven days before the full moon, since all the rituals of the water spirits are performed during the full moon.

On the third day of the purification, the following should be written with a red pen on a white sheet:

I (write name) son of (mother's name) and (father's name) born on (date of birth). I come to you, oh divine mother, goddess of water, Yemaya, so that you grant me the hand of one of your daughters so that I can take her as a wife and that you grant me wealth and success in all my endeavors.

After that the letter has to be signed and then the ring finger of the right hand has to be pricked with a pin, letting three drops of blood fall on the letter. Now you have to trace a pentagram with said ring finger on the card, using the blood from the wound.

Now you have to place the letter at the bottom of the clay pot and put the nine kola nuts on top of said letter. Then the practitioner should go to the sea or a nearby river at midnight.

Clay pot © Luksyol

After standing at the water's edge, the clay pot should be raised forward with both hands facing the water, while saying the following words:

Ehuu, Ehuu, Ehuu |

Oh, divine mother, Yemaya, goddess of water.
Open the doors of Pandemonium for me.
Accept my letter.
Accept the alliance that I wish to enter into with
you.
Grant me the hand of one of your daughters so
that I can take her as my wife.
Make my life prosperous and that I succeed in
all my endeavors.
In return I promise to fulfill the task you order
me to perform.

After that the practitioner should wade in waist deep into the water and place the clay pot on the surface. Immediately afterwards, he returns to the shore walking backwards and leave the place without turning their heads.

On the night of the seventh day, the practitioner must go to the same place where he performed the first ritual, with all the other objects on the list. As always, he must be dressed in the ceremonial robe, with the white scarf wrapped around his head like a turban.

Now the fruits and the bottles of gin and soft drinks must be introduced inside the pumpkin. Immediately afterwards, the hundred grams of rice are also poured inside. Then a little *Mami Water* perfume is sprayed around the top edges of the gourd, both the inside and outside edges.

Immediately afterwards, the two silver rings are also sprayed with the *Mami Water perfume* and inserted into the pumpkin. Then the practitioner should trace a circle with *Bint El Sudan* talc around himself near the water.

But the gourd must remain outside said circle and must remain just where the waves of the sea can reach it or very close to the river water, in case the ritual is not taking place at the edge of the sea. The important thing is that said gourd must be in contact with water.

Now the practitioner must spray the six white candles and the six red candles with the *Mami Water perfume* and then completely spray himself with said perfume. Immediately afterwards, the candles should be placed clockwise on the circle formed with the talcum powder.

Hollowed out gourd © Djoliba

You must place the candles alternating colors. That is, a white candle and a red one. Another white candle followed by another red, until the circle is complete. Then the candles must be lit following the same clockwise direction.

Then the following mantra should be recited 21 times, looking towards the sea:

Extrantum, Krantum, Frantum | [5]

Immediately afterwards, the practitioner must pronounce the following words:

Yemaya, Yemaya, Yemaya.
Goddess of water I come again tonight so that
you grant me the hand of one of your daughters,
so that I can marry her to obtain wealth and
success in all my endeavors.
Please grant me this wish that I ask of you.

Then the practitioner must remain attentive to the water for fifteen minutes. During that time several things can happen. There may be a sudden strange calm or a strong wind may start to blow. And it is

---

[5] Mantra 05

also possible that someone or something emerges from the water and goes towards the practitioner. In any case, he must be previously prepared to handle any incident.

After fifteen minutes, the practitioner must get out the circle and leave the place without looking back, leaving all the objects of the ritual in that place, without touching anything.

PACT WITH THE GODDESS *SHEKINAH*

The goddess *Shekinah* is one of the oldest spirits in the universe. She is even older than *Yemaya* and most of the god's known and unknown to man. She is the one who rides on top of *Leviathan*, the legendary dragon with seven heads and ten horns, holding the golden cup that contains the juice of wisdom and knowledge.

Divine Mother *Shekinah* © Frederica Underwood

And it was she who gave Adam and Eve the fruit of knowledge, opening their eyes to make them see the illusory world or *Maya* in which they were immersed. And then for the first time they realized that they were naked. The problem is that the church has deliberately hidden the truth, altering it or simply removing it from the history books.

Such was the obsession of the church to maintain absolute power over the people that thousands of defenseless women perished at the stake and millions of books were destroyed. In this way, knowledge and secrets of incalculable value were lost forever. That was a great irreparable loss for all humanity.

The Babylonians, the Sumerians, the Egyptians, the Mayans and other older cultures and civilizations knew the keys to communicate with the ancient gods, long before the arrival of Christianity. And thanks to the help and knowledge obtained from those gods and goddesses, these cultures were so glorious and built buildings that remain standing even after thousands of years.

The ritual described in the next pages will allow the practitioner to contact the goddess *Shekinah,* one of the most ancient forces in the universe, to obtain her favors. It is a relatively simple but extremely powerful ritual. And to carry it out, you will only need the following objects:

1. Forty-four coconuts.
2. A tray big enough to hold all forty-four coconuts.
3. A white ceremonial robe.
4. A red scarf.
5. A *Mami Wata* perfume.
6. A white candle.
7. Several bottles of skimmed milk.

After gathering these objects, the next thing will be fasting for seven days. And during that period of fasting it is obligatory to maintain a sattvic diet, avoiding meat and fish also avoiding foods that contain garlic or onion. Alcohol and other toxic substances should be avoided, as well as any type of sexual activity. The practitioner must distance himself from the society and sleep in the ritual room.

On the night of the seventh day, the practitioner should wash his body using only skimmed milk. Then he must appear at 24:00 on a lonely beach, being dressed in the white ceremonial tunic and the red scarf tied at the waist.

Then the practitioner must begin to perfume the body with the *Mami Water* perfume, starting from the feet to the head. Then you must spread said perfume in the four cardinal points and then spread towards the sky and towards the earth.

Now the candle must be stuck in the sand on the beach and light it. Then you take the tray containing the forty-four coconuts and move towards the water. Then you must count the waves that come to extinguish in the sand. If the practitioner is a woman, she must count to seven waves before entering the water. And if it is a man then he must count to nine waves.

After counting the waves you have to enter the sea, submerging up to your waist. Then the tray containing the coconuts is placed gently on top of the water and is held with the left hand so that it does not sink. While with the right hand the following mudra is performed:

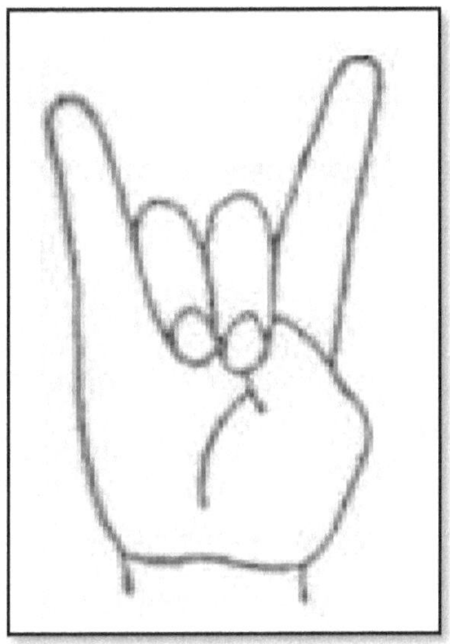

Mudra that is performed with the right hand

Now you have to recite the following mantra, with your right hand raised. Women have to recite it for seven times. And if it is a male practitioner, then he must recite it nine times.

Levia-Suquca-Yekemawah |
Shekinah-Yekemawah |
Sucuka-Yekemawah |

After reciting the mantra, then one has to say the following words, keeping the hand up:

Oh, Divine Mother of the oceans, Shekinah.
Oh high priestess, you who rule and sit on Leviathan, seven-headed dragon.
Me (say your full name), son of (say your mother's name) and (say your father's name)
I have come here today to achieve what I could not achieve on my own, oh divine mother.
Give me money and wealth. Make me rich and prosperous.
And in return I will give you (name what you will give in return)

After that you have to lower your hand and drop the tray containing the offering. After fifteen minutes you have to get out of the water walking backwards and leave the place. That night you have to sleep in the room for rituals, where the altar of *Mami Wata* is located.

---

[6] Mantra 06

This ritual has to be carried out on a very secluded and lonely beach, because when the goddess *Shekinah* appears there is usually lightning and thunder, accompanied by a huge storm. Then the waters part and she rises to the surface riding the *Leviathan*.

The creature on which the goddess sits resembles a cross between a serpent and a seven-headed, legged dragon. That creature is as huge as a mountain and its seven heads are so big that they could swallow a whole car very easily.

It is an apocalyptic vision that would make even the bravest of humans faint with fear. It is not recommended to carry out the present ritual at all if the practitioner has not previously established a solid connection with the spirits of the water. Otherwise he will have to face the consequences.

CONJURING THE MERMAID *JACQUELINE*

The mermaid named *Jacqueline* is one of the princesses who rule the coasts of West Africa. And his power is especially enormous. Their rituals are generally dangerous and are not recommended for beginners. Her way of manifesting is usually totally unpredictable. She can take any form. So their rituals are not intended for those who are new to evoking water spirits.

This ritual should not be performed lightly, if the practitioner is not fully prepared to assume any consequences. There is no remedy in the world to exorcise this spirit once it has been conjured. But if you are prepared enough for calmly and courageously receive Princess Jacqueline and perform the ritual correctly, then there will be no need for any further exorcism.

There are several rituals to conjure up this spirit, but I cannot mention them all in this book. So I will only give the instructions about the shortest and simplest ritual that the practitioner will use to make that princess of the water come. But first you must get the items from the following list:

1. A black rosary.
2. A bottle of red wine.
3. A glass.
4. Three black candles.
5. Three red candles.
6. A black robe.
7. A red scarf.

Once you have gathered these objects, you must first carry out the seven days of regulatory purification. On the seventh day of the purification, that is to say, the Friday of the full moon, the ritual can be carried out. And the most interesting thing about this spell is that it is performed in the bathroom of the practitioner's home, without having to go to the sea.

At twelve o'clock at night, the practitioner should get dressed with the black robe, tying the red scarf on the waist. No undergarments or jewelry should be worn on any part of the body. He has to fill the glass with red wine and place the rosary inside the glass. Then he enters the bathroom and closes the door.

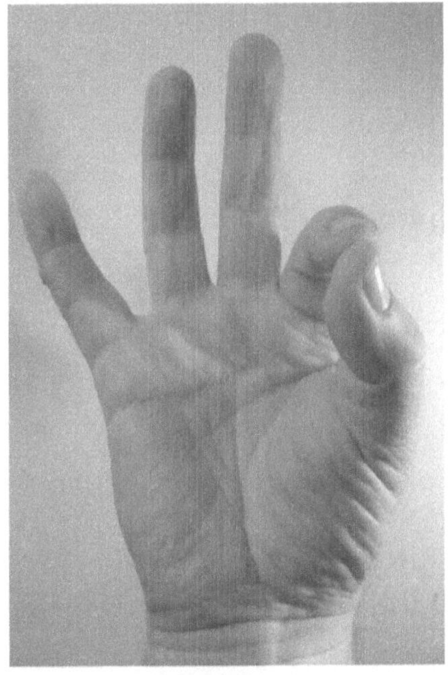
Gyan Mudra © Detevige.com

Once the glass is placed in the center of the instance, now the six candles must be placed in all corners of the bathroom and they must be lit. There should be no other light in the bathroom apart from candles. Then the practitioner takes the glass with both hands and presents it in the four directions, starting with the north, south, east and west. Then he places the glass on the floor, in the center of the bathroom. Then he stands in front of the glass and perform the *Gyan Mudra* with the right hand.

While performing the *Gyan Mudra* he should stare at the glass and recite the following words:

Annibass
Asmodeus
Shamadd
Amimonn |
Extrantuum, Extrantuum, Extrantuum | [7]

After pronouncing these words he must drink half the wine from the glass. Then he has to make a wish and pour some wine down the toilet. For example:

Oh Jacqueline. I call you because I want you to bring wealth and prosperity to my life.

Every time he repeats the wish he should pour some wine down the toilet. The practitioner must repeat that act six times. Then he should pour some of the

---

[7] Mantra 07

remaining wine into the palm of his hand and wet the head with it. He put a little wine back and wet his head. The third time he must pour the rest of the wine from the glass into the palm of the hand and wet his head again.

Now he must break the glass by crashing it hard against the ground. He picks up the rosary and put it on his neck. Then he immediately leaves the bathroom, leaving the candles burning. The practitioner must sleep in the ritual room without changing his clothes.

EPILOGUE

Now that you have reached the last section of this book, it is important that you know some essential details to keep in mind when carrying out the rituals of the *Mami Wata* spirits. To guarantee success, it is absolutely necessary to adopt a certain way of life and develop a series of qualities. Some of them are silence, discretion, neatness and chastity.

Silence: There is a tremendous power only accessible by those who are able to keep their mouths shut. There is power in silence, but that power disappears or weakens every time we talk to other people especially when it comes to banal and superfluous conversations. Talking should be avoided as much as possible, unless absolutely necessary.

Have you ever wondered why quiet and reserved people are the most interesting? Well, something similar also happens in magic, but in a mystical sense. When we keep silent we accumulate power, especially if we are doing a spiritual practice.

But every time we speak that power slips away. Because there are many ways a person can lose their psychic energy, and one of those ways is through the mouth. For this reason, hermits, ascetics and other people seclude themselves in isolated places, to distance themselves from society.

Discretion: Everyone wants to have power and wealth, but only a few people are capable of keeping a secret. As soon as you start getting paranormal experiences after practicing the rituals in this book you will rush to tell other people about it, which would be a serious mistake on your part.

Water spirits are very secretive and love to remain incognito. They are not happy that their presence in our world is perceived or known by third parties. And that is one of the conditions that you must accept and respect when you decide to conjure these spirits.

No one should know that you are performing the rituals in this book. You mustn't even let that be suspected or let people know that you have the slightest interest in those spirits. If possible, stay away from environments where they are mentioned or discussed, lest they inadvertently elicit information from you.

The only person you can talk to about the details of the ritual is your guru. But if you don't have any guru, then you can send me an email to clarify any doubt about the rituals or to request some kind of guidance. You should not include any personal information in the email, such as your name, your gender or your geographical location.

Neatness: The water spirits are possibly the neatest spirits I've ever come across. They are true fans of cleanliness and order. Having white as their favorite color, they demand that this be also preferred by their followers. The room where these spirits are worshiped or the place where they regularly go should be completely white.

The sheets, curtains and other objects in said room must be white. It is recommended that there are no unnecessary objects in the room, apart from the bed and the altar. Because *Mami Wata* spirits are allergic to a long list of things, including leather objects and any sharp item.

Most of the adherents of these water spirits are also obliged to dress strictly in white on a regular basis, or at least during the days that they are going to receive the visit of the spirit.

In addition, the followers must also adopt the same neatness that characterizes the spirits they worship. And their clothes must be immaculately white and remain clean at all times. New or freshly washed clothes should be worn every day, without ever repeating the clothes worn the day before. At least they shouldn't be used without washing them first.

Followers should also wash thoroughly each time after defecating while carrying out purification rituals and should never go to bed at night without showering. The practitioner should take care of his dental hygiene, cut his nails, take care of the beard and always keep himself attractive to please his spiritual lover.

Chastity: This is perhaps the most important requirement for success in the spirit evocation rituals of this book. Chastity has always been very important, not only in the art of magic, but also in the performance of any significant spiritual task.

Before performing any *Mami Wata* ritual, a purification period must be carried out and during this period chastity must be maintained on a mental, vocal and physical level. This means that you should avoid thinking about sex, talking about it or doing it in any way, including masturbation.

Even if, while sleeping, the practitioner has wet dreams and ejaculates, then it should be understood that the purification period has been interrupted and has to be started all over again.

Another equally important quality that must be developed by the practitioner is courage. I have deliberately omitted the ways in which these water spirits present themselves during the performance of the rituals, or in the days immediately following.

I have omitted that part to prevent the practitioner from performing the rituals with fear in his heart. It only seems necessary to me to point out that some of the appearances that these spirits adopt can be truly terrifying, beyond the reach of the human imagination.

But their terrifying appearances do not necessarily indicate that they are spirits of a dark or negative nature. It's just one of their favorite ways they measure a practitioner's level of bravery. Because bravery is one of the most valued qualities in the spiritual world and the spirits take it very seriously.

They have to be sure that the practitioner is really worthwhile and lives up to their expectations. In fact, while the practitioner performs the conjuration, the spirits are constantly watching intently, even though they remain invisible. They are very detailed and demanding and do not allow the slightest mistake to be made during the execution of the ritual.

So before you decide to perform the rituals in this book, it is wise to familiarize yourself with them first. One has to master the pronunciation of the mantras and memorize them completely. That way you will avoid making mistakes when the time comes to perform the ritual.

It is also important to be clear beforehand exactly what you want from the spirit you are conjuring. When the spirit comes, the practitioner has to be brief, clear and concise. And above all he must try not to let his voice tremble. It should always be remembered that anything that appears during the execution of the rituals or in the days after, is not there to harm you, even if it has a threatening attitude.

Now I only have to say for the last time that it is highly important to reflect deeply before performing any of the rituals that I offer in this book, because afterwards it is not possible to go back. And there is no ritual or exorcism that can rid you of the spirits you will find here, once you have conjured them.

For my part, I only offer conjuration rituals and I do not have exorcism rituals. And just because I do offer those conjuring rituals doesn't necessarily mean I´m encouraging people to perform them. All I do is offer knowledge and what each person does with that information is entirely their business.

My warnings may seem repetitive and some readers will think that my intention is to discourage people from performing the rituals, which is completely incorrect. Wise and prudent readers should take these warnings as the advice and recommendations of a much more experienced friend who only wants the best for them.

Because it is necessary for the practitioner to know exactly what he is dealing with before entering a specific field of magic, that way, whatever happens, he can't blame anyone else but himself.

For any questions or need for guidance, readers can send an email to the following address: benny.torres@outlook.com I will try to reply as soon as I can.

To listen to the audio pronunciations of the different mantras in this book, you can access the following URL address: https://youtube.com/@benny.torres

www.ingramcontent.com/pod-product-compliance
Lightning Source LLC
Chambersburg PA
CBHW031430150726
47989CB00002B/878